Black Leaders in the Civil Rights Movement

FREEDOM
RIGHTS
DO YOU !! HEAR !!
YOU CAN'T KEEP ME QUIET

Black LEADERS in the Civil Rights Movement

A BLACK HISTORY BOOK FOR KIDS

Glenda Armand

Illustrations by María Perera

ROCKRIDGE PRESS

For general information on our other products and services or to obtain technical support, please contact our Customer Care Department within the United States at (866) 744-2665, or outside the United States at (510) 253-0500.

Rockridge Press publishes its books in a variety of electronic and print formats. Some content that appears in print may not be available in electronic books, and vice versa.

Series Designer: Will Mack
Interior and Cover Designer: Lisa Schreiber
Art Producer: Tom Hood
Editor: Barbara J. Isenberg
Production Editor: Mia Moran
Production Manager: Jose Olivera

Illustrations © María Perera, 2021.
Author photograph courtesy of Valerie Ciernick.

Paperback ISBN: 978-1-64876-445-5
eBook ISBN: 978-1-64876-446-2
R1

Printed in China

This book is dedicated to my great-great grandfather, Victor Jones Sr., who was born into slavery in 1845 in Vacherie, Louisiana. He lived a life of purpose and dignity and on January 15, 1928, died a free man.

Contents

Introduction

The civil rights movement was an organized effort by **African** Americans to claim the rights that the U.S. government had denied them.

The Declaration of Independence of the United States of America states: "All men are created equal [. . .] with certain unalienable rights, [and] among these are life, liberty, and the pursuit of happiness." Yet, when the Declaration of Independence was signed on July 4, 1776, about 500,000 African Americans remained **enslaved**. **Slavery** allowed black people to be bought and sold as if they were property. For black people in the United States, the fight for freedom and independence continued.

Many found a way to be free. Some escaped their captors in the middle of the night. Countless died trying. Some saved money for years to buy their freedom. No price was too great. They never gave up. In 1865, slavery was **abolished**. Four million African Americans began life as a new people—a free people—but in a hostile land.

The first years of freedom were challenging. All of a sudden, freed men and women had to find jobs, housing, and education. But they were free. That first generation navigated their way through unfamiliar and dangerous territory, leaving a path for their children to follow.

Their children knew what slavery had been like for their parents. But they had their own struggle. Freedom had been won, but the battle for equal treatment and the rights of citizenship had just begun. Yet, even as they struggled for basic rights, this generation of African Americans produced the first post-slavery doctors, teachers, scientists, and business owners.

It was the next generation, the grandchildren of the freed men and women, who created the civil rights movement. They were the second generation born free, but they heard sad stories about slavery from their grandparents. They also understood that, although free, they were far from equal in U.S. society. They knew that true freedom could not exist with **Jim Crow laws**, which denied their equality. They could not live in peace as long as **racist** groups like the **Ku Klux Klan** threatened their jobs and lives.

This generation of 15 million people rose up to fight for the rights they deserved as citizens—their civil rights. From the early 1950s to the late 1960s, thousands of African Americans struggled to make the United States live up to its promise. They participated in marches, **sit-ins**, and **boycotts**. They fought oppression by speaking up for themselves and with silent **resistance**. Some endured physical attacks, imprisonment, and death. We will never know all of their names, sacrifices, and brave deeds. But from among them, many leaders arose.

In this book, you will get to know 15 of those leaders. You will read about their unique journeys that led them to the forefront of the civil rights movement. What made them stand out? What made them willing to give their all? In these pages, you will hear them answer in their own voices.

You will find, as you read, that African Americans have referred to themselves in different ways over the years: colored, Negro, black, Afro-American. These terms were not considered to be negative when they were used. Language is constantly changing.

The civil rights movement was made up largely of African Americans fighting for their own rights. But people of every background joined as allies as African Americans fought to claim their right to life, liberty, and the pursuit of happiness.

FREEDOM
RIGHTS
YOU CAN'T KEEP ME QUIET
DO YOU !! HEAR !!

Claudette COLVIN

{ 1939–Present }

Claudette Colvin was only fifteen years old when she was faced with the decision to stand up to **injustice**. But she was ready. In school, she had been learning African American history. She had studied the U.S. **Constitution**. And she had experienced **prejudice** in her everyday life. When the time came, Claudette summoned her courage, spoke up for herself, and set into motion a series of events that would lead to lasting change.

In 1947, when Claudette was eight years old, she moved with her family from the tiny town of Pine Level, Alabama, to Montgomery, the state capital. Claudette was smart and curious and loved to read. She soon learned that in Montgomery, black and white people lived by different sets of laws. Claudette questioned why she was not allowed to try on dresses, shoes, or hats at clothing stores. She wondered why black families couldn't play or sit on benches in the city park.

Day after day and year after year, Claudette witnessed the unfair ways in which black people were treated.

Segregation laws called for black and white people to be kept apart from each other in theaters, in stores, and on buses.

While she was a junior at all-black Booker T. Washington High School, Claudette received answers to some of her questions. Her favorite teachers spent the entire month of February teaching students about the history and achievements of their African ancestors. The students learned about slavery and the brave people, like Harriet Tubman and Sojourner Truth, who fought against it. Claudette learned that the **discrimination** she experienced was slavery's terrible **legacy**.

Studying the U.S. Constitution gave Claudette hope that things would get better. Claudette believed that the rights guaranteed in the Constitution applied to African Americans, too. Soon she would be challenged to put what she believed into practice.

On Wednesday, March 2, 1955, Claudette and three friends caught the city bus after school. There were separate sections for white and black people. White people sat in the front of the bus and black people in the back. Claudette and her friends paid their fare and sat in the row behind the empty white section. The bus continued on, picking up passengers.

Soon, all of the seats for white people were full. When a young white woman got on the bus, that meant the white section had to be expanded. The bus driver ordered Claudette and her friends to move back. While her three classmates obeyed the driver, Claudette remained

> **"HISTORY KEPT ME STUCK TO MY SEAT. I FELT THE HAND OF HARRIET TUBMAN PUSHING DOWN ON ONE SHOULDER AND SOJOURNER TRUTH PUSHING DOWN ON THE OTHER."**

seated. The white woman stood beside Claudette's seat, waiting.

Later, Claudette would retell the story of what happened next:

"Why are you still sitting there?" asked the bus driver.

Claudette did not respond.

"Get up, gal!" the bus driver ordered.

When Claudette still refused to move, the driver called the police. Two police officers boarded the bus and stood over Claudette.

"Aren't you going to get up?" one of the officers demanded.

"No, sir," Claudette responded. "It's my constitutional right to sit here as much as that lady. I paid my fare. It's my constitutional right!"

The officers dragged Claudette, kicking and screaming, off the bus. They handcuffed her and drove her to the police station. Claudette was arrested and shoved into a jail cell. She was sobbing and praying when her mother and **pastor** came to get her out of jail.

Black people in Montgomery were outraged when they heard the news of Claudette's arrest. Enough was enough.

It was time to end segregation on buses. A group of black leaders went to meet with the chief of police. One of those leaders was a young pastor named Martin Luther King Jr. (page 61).

Unfortunately, the meeting between the black leaders and the city officials did not bring about a change in the bus laws. In a Montgomery courthouse, Claudette was tried and found guilty of the crime of assaulting, or harming, a police officer. She was ordered to pay a fine and to "stay out of trouble." Still, people in the black community called Claudette brave and said that she had done a wonderful thing.

Claudette met with Rosa Parks (page 7), a secretary for the National Association for the Advancement of Colored People (NAACP). The NAACP's mission was to fight for fair treatment of African Americans. Parks encouraged Claudette to tell her story to young members of the NAACP. Black leaders briefly considered calling for a boycott—that is, for African Americans to refuse to ride the buses until the laws were changed. But, mostly because she was so young, they decided that Claudette would not be the right spokesperson for a boycott. However, Claudette's experience sparked something even bigger.

Fred Gray, a lawyer, filed a lawsuit against Montgomery and its mayor, W. A. Gayle, on behalf of Claudette and three other black women who had been mistreated on a city bus: Aurelia Browder, Susie McDonald, and Mary Louise Smith. The trial date was set for May 11, 1956.

When her turn came to testify, Claudette spoke thoughtfully and forcefully.

The case, *Browder v. Gayle,* made it all the way to the U.S. Supreme Court, the highest court in the land. On December 20, 1956, the Court found that the bus law did not treat people equally. It ruled that the law was **unconstitutional** and must be repealed, or canceled.

Claudette's brave act did not spark the Montgomery Bus Boycott. However, it did lead to the Supreme Court decision that brought the boycott to an end. *Browder v. Gayle* gave civil rights **activists** the legal power to challenge segregation laws throughout the South. Claudette's actions also inspired countless other African Americans to stand up to injustice through nonviolence and legal action. Claudette proved that, in the quest for justice, it was possible for even a teenager to lead the way.

EXPLORE MORE! Read more about Claudette in *Claudette Colvin: Twice Toward Justice* by Phillip Hoose. In this book, you will learn about Claudette's experience in her own words.

DID YOU KNOW? Historian Carter G. Woodson began the celebration of Negro History Week on February 7, 1926. The month of February is still dedicated to African American history.

Rosa PARKS

{ 1913–2005 }

Every time Rosa Parks boarded a bus, she received a painful reminder that African Americans did not have equal rights in Montgomery, Alabama. Black people could only sit in the back of the bus. When all seats were taken, black people had to stand and give their seats to white people. But, thanks to Rosa Parks, these unfair rules would eventually come to an end.

Born Rosa Louise McCauley, in Tuskegee, Alabama, Rosa had **European**, **Indigenous**, and African ancestors. After her parents separated, Rosa, her mother, and her brother went to live with her mother's parents on their farm in Pine Level, Alabama.

When she reached school age, Rosa walked with other African American children to a one-room schoolhouse. Each morning, a school bus full of white children passed them by. That bus provided Rosa's first lesson on segregation. The white children on the bus were headed to a modern school with new supplies and equipment. In Rosa's schoolhouse, there were never enough paper, pencils, or books. Rosa and her fellow students didn't even have desks.

Rosa's grandparents, who had once been enslaved, helped Rosa understand segregation. They told her how her African ancestors had been brought to the United States against their will and sold to the owners of large farms, called **plantations**. The Africans worked for no pay and were often treated very badly.

Fortunately for Rosa's grandparents, slavery ended when they were young. However, after slavery was abolished, some white people formed a group called the Ku Klux Klan (KKK) that committed acts of **violence** against black people. The KKK did not want black and white people to live together as equals. To defend his family against this hateful group, Rosa's grandfather kept a shotgun by his side.

At the age of eleven, Rosa enrolled in a school known as "Miss White's School" in the nearby city of Montgomery. It was founded by white teachers for black girls. Rosa was an excellent student. She was treated with dignity and respect and was taught to set her sights high. And she did.

As a young woman, Rosa became involved in the civil rights movement. At the age of nineteen, she married Raymond Parks, who was a member of the National Association for the Advancement of Colored People (NAACP). Raymond thought it was too dangerous for Rosa to join the group. The NAACP meetings had to be held in secret because the KKK often attacked NAACP members.

However, Rosa had inherited her grandfather's bravery. She joined the NAACP and became the secretary for the Montgomery **chapter**.

As the head of the NAACP's youth group, Rosa especially enjoyed mentoring young people. She met Claudette Colvin (page 1), who had been arrested for refusing to give up her bus seat. Rosa was no stranger to run-ins with bus drivers.

Rosa remembered one incident very well. On a rainy day, she had boarded a bus and paid her fare. Then the driver ordered her to get off the bus and reboard through the back door, as the law required. When Rosa refused, the driver grabbed her and put her off the bus. As the bus pulled away, Rosa remembered what the driver looked like. She wanted to make sure she never rode his bus again.

Now, many years later, Rosa was happy to help raise money to hire a lawyer to defend Claudette in court. Rosa was disappointed when black leaders decided that this was not the right time to call for a bus boycott. However, just nine months later, the right time came. And it was because of Rosa.

On December 1, 1955, Rosa boarded a bus, paid her fare, and sat in the row directly behind the "white" section. Then Rosa noticed that the driver was the same man who had left her standing in the rain 12 years earlier. As the bus traveled along its regular route, the section reserved for white people filled up. That meant more rows had to be included in the white section. The driver demanded

"I HAVE LEARNED OVER THE YEARS THAT WHEN ONE'S MIND IS MADE UP, THIS DIMINISHES FEAR; KNOWING WHAT MUST BE DONE DOES AWAY WITH FEAR."

that Rosa and the three other people in her row give up their seats.

While the other three got up, Rosa responded, "I don't think I should have to stand up." This time, the driver did not throw Rosa off the bus. He called the police to arrest her.

Black leaders had been looking for someone to lead the **desegregation** movement in Montgomery. Although Claudette had been arrested months earlier, the leaders worried that she was too young to represent the boycott. When Rosa was arrested, the leaders agreed that she was the one. They called for a boycott. Black people in Montgomery immediately stopped riding the city buses.

Day after day, empty buses rolled down Montgomery's streets. Black people shared rides, rode horses, and walked to work and school. Since black people made up the majority of bus riders, the city lost money. Throughout the boycott, Rosa faced threats and harassment. She and her husband were fired from their jobs.

Finally, after 381 days, the boycott ended when the U.S. Supreme Court ruled that Montgomery's bus laws were unconstitutional. There would be no more white sections and black sections on city buses.

Rosa did not stop fighting for equal treatment. Eventually, she and her husband moved to Detroit, Michigan. Rosa began traveling across the country to give her support and time to civil rights causes and events. She established a scholarship fund for high school seniors who were going to college. And in 1987, she co-founded the Rosa and Raymond Parks Institute for Self Development, an organization that still serves children in Detroit. In 1999, Rosa was awarded the Congressional Gold Medal, the highest honor given to someone who does not hold an official office.

Rosa will always be remembered for her brave act of refusing to give up her seat on a Montgomery bus. That simple act sparked the first and largest boycott of the civil rights movement. However, before and after the boycott, Rosa led a life dedicated to obtaining justice for black people. She showed us how one determined person can make a difference.

EXPLORE MORE! Step into history! At the Henry Ford Museum in Dearborn, Michigan, you can board the very same bus that Rosa was riding when she was arrested.

DID YOU KNOW? The NAACP was founded in 1909 in response to ongoing violence against black people. It is the largest civil rights organization in the nation. Its mission is to eliminate race-based discrimination.

Thurgood MARSHALL

{ 1908–1993 }

Public schools, like city buses, were a key battleground in the fight for civil rights. When Thurgood Marshall was a child, he was forced to attend all-black schools. When he grew up, Thurgood became a lawyer. In his most famous case, *Brown v. Board of Education*, Thurgood argued that public schools should be **integrated**. Separate was not equal.

Thurgood was born "Thoroughgood" Marshall, in Baltimore, Maryland. The second son of William and Norma Marshall, he was named after his grandfather, who had escaped from slavery.

Thurgood was wise beyond his years. While in second grade, he presented his first "case" to a jury of his teacher and family. He wanted to change his name. It was too long to write, he argued. It should be spelled the way it was already pronounced. The seven-year-old won the case of *Thoroughgood v. Thurgood*. His name was spelled "Thurgood" from then on.

Thurgood showed other signs of his future career. His father often took his sons to the local courthouse to watch trials. Later, at the dinner table, they discussed what they had seen and heard. They debated the legal issues. Mr. Marshall challenged his sons on the points they made. Thurgood was always determined to prove his case.

In high school, Thurgood was an above-average student and a star member of the debate team. But he also liked to have fun and play practical jokes, so Thurgood often found himself in the principal's office. Fortunately for him, the principal had a unique way of disciplining him. Every time he got into trouble, he had to memorize part of the U.S. Constitution. By the time he graduated with honors in 1925, Thurgood had memorized the entire document. That knowledge would serve him well.

While a student at Lincoln University in Pennsylvania, a college founded for black men, Thurgood had his first experience with peaceful protest. He and his friends often went to the movies. However, at the theater, they were not allowed to sit in the seats on the main floor. They paid the same price for their tickets as white moviegoers, but they were forced to sit in the far-away balcony.

One day, Thurgood and his friends decided to protest this unfair treatment. A large group of students got together and went to the theater. When they paid for their tickets, the students went inside and took seats on the main floor. The usher demanded that they get up and go upstairs to the balcony. Thurgood and his friends did not move.

Surprisingly, the police were not called, and the boys were allowed to watch the movie. From then on, when the Lincoln students went to the theater, they sat wherever they wanted. This experience taught Thurgood the power of **direct action**. Twenty years later, activists in the civil rights movement would successfully use direct action such as boycotts and sit-ins to achieve their goal of equal treatment.

After graduating in 1930, Thurgood applied to the University of Maryland School of Law in his hometown. Despite having excellent grades, Thurgood was rejected because of his race. After this disappointment, he studied law at Howard University, an all-black college. The law professors at Howard were also lawyers. Thurgood helped try real cases in court.

When he studied the Constitution further, it became clear to Thurgood that all Americans were not receiving the equal treatment that the Constitution guaranteed. His mission would be to right this wrong. Thurgood graduated from Howard *magna cum laude* (with great distinction) in 1933.

He went to work for the National Association for the Advancement of Colored People (NAACP). When black people came to the NAACP with complaints of discrimination, Thurgood used his legal skills to help them.

"A CHILD BORN TO A BLACK MOTHER IN A STATE LIKE MISSISSIPPI [. . .] HAS EXACTLY THE SAME RIGHTS AS A WHITE BABY BORN TO THE WEALTHIEST PERSON IN THE UNITED STATES."

Thurgood presented 32 cases before the U.S. Supreme Court. He won all but three cases.

But it was the case of *Brown v. Board of Education of Topeka* that established Thurgood's place in history and earned him the title "Mr. Civil Rights." The case went to the Supreme Court after the father of a nine-year-old girl named Linda Brown tried to enroll his daughter at Sumner Elementary School. Sumner was an all-white school near the Browns' home in Topeka, Kansas.

Brown felt it was wrong for his daughter to have to walk past Sumner and go across town to the all-black school. Sumner Elementary refused to enroll Linda, and her father turned to the NAACP for help.

About 60 years earlier, in *Plessy v. Ferguson*, the Supreme Court had ruled that racial segregation laws for public facilities were constitutional as long as the segregated facilities were equal in quality. This **doctrine** came to be known as "separate but equal." Thurgood argued that schools for black children were in poorer condition than those for white children. The Supreme Court agreed. It ruled that having separate schools for black and white children was unconstitutional.

Some historians say that Thurgood's victory in *Brown v. Board of Education* marked the true beginning of the civil rights movement. It showed people fighting for their rights that they had two powerful weapons: peaceful resistance (direct action) and the law. Thurgood had used both.

Other cases Thurgood argued before the Supreme Court produced rulings that have had lasting benefits, especially for poor people and African Americans. Those cases have made it easier for black people to exercise their right to vote (*Smith v. Allwright*), made it unlawful to force someone to confess to a crime (*Lyons v. State of Oklahoma*), and ensured that people accused of a crime receive a fair trial (*Patton v. State of Mississippi*).

Brown v. Board of Education also had a great effect on Thurgood's career. In 1967, President Lyndon B. Johnson appointed him to be the first African American justice to serve on the Supreme Court. Thurgood sat on the Supreme Court for 24 years. In his rulings, he always stressed the need for equal treatment of all citizens.

EXPLORE MORE! One of Thurgood's classmates at Lincoln University was Langston Hughes, who became a famous poet. You can read one of Langston's poems, called "My People," online.

DID YOU KNOW? The U.S. Constitution is the oldest governing document of any nation today. At only five pages long, it is also the shortest. It only takes about 30 minutes to read. Can you memorize the Preamble, or opening section?

NAACP
SNCC
SCEF

Ella BAKER

{ 1903–1986 }

Ella Josephine Baker's name is not as familiar as the names of the people she worked with. Two of the people who depended on Ella's skills, advice, and knowledge were Martin Luther King Jr. (page 61) and Rosa Parks (page 7). Ella did not mind being in the background. Her only goal was to make change happen.

Ella was born in Norfolk, Virginia, the second of three children. In 1910, Norfolk had a **riot** in which white people attacked black shipyard workers. After the riot, Ella's family did not feel safe in Norfolk. They went to live in North Carolina on her grandparents' farm. The farm had once been part of the plantation on which her grandparents had been enslaved. Ella listened attentively as Grandmother Bet told stories of being whipped and beaten.

Ella's family valued hard work and kindness. After her grandparents were freed, they worked, saved, and sacrificed until they were able to buy their farm for $250, a large amount of money in those days. On their farm, they raised fruit, vegetables, and cattle, which they shared with their neighbors. Ella's grandfather was also a Baptist minister. Her mother was a caregiver. Ella often joined her mother as she walked from house to house, caring for the sick and needy.

Ella left home as a ninth grader to attend Shaw Academy, a **boarding school** run by Shaw University in Raleigh, North Carolina. An outstanding student, Ella graduated as the **valedictorian** of her class. After receiving her diploma, Ella continued her education at Shaw University. It was the first African American college to accept women. To support herself and pay her tuition, Ella worked as a waitress and chemistry lab assistant. Despite having two jobs, Ella managed to excel in college. When she graduated from Shaw in 1927, she was once again at the top of her class.

After graduation, Ella moved to New York City. For the next five decades, she played a key role in three of the most important organizations of the civil rights movement: the National Association for the Advancement of Colored People (NAACP), the Southern **Christian** Leadership Conference (SCLC), and the Student **Nonviolent** Coordinating Committee (SNCC).

In 1938, Ella began her involvement with the NAACP as a secretary. In 1943, she became a director, the highest-ranking woman in the group. Ella made it a top priority to give women more power in the organization.

As a national director, Ella traveled throughout the South, raising money, recruiting members, and starting local chapters. Ella was successful because she earned the trust and respect of the people she met. She slept in their homes, ate at their tables, and spoke in their churches. Ella especially welcomed young people. They were eager to help the NAACP in its mission to eliminate the Jim Crow laws that discriminated against black people.

While working with the NAACP in New York, Ella became interested in helping the people involved in the Montgomery Bus Boycott. She returned to the South to help the leaders of that boycott create a new organization called the Southern Christian Leadership Conference. This group would call for direct action throughout the South, such as boycotts and sit-ins.

SCLC's first project was a voter registration campaign. Ella believed that voting was a key to freedom. It was a way to put people in office who believed in equal rights for all. But for years, it had been difficult, even dangerous, for black people to register, or sign up, and vote. Armed men sometimes showed up to turn black people away from voting places. When SCLC made it easier and safer, more African Americans voted.

In 1960, Ella heard about some black college students in Greensboro, North Carolina, who were staging a sit-in at a Woolworth lunch counter, where black people had been refused service. Ella wanted to help. On behalf of SCLC, she called for a meeting of student leaders from all across the South. More than 100 college students showed up for the meeting. From that meeting a new organization was born: the Student Nonviolent Coordinating Committee. In

"UNTIL THE KILLING OF BLACK MEN, BLACK MOTHERS' SONS, BECOMES AS IMPORTANT TO THE REST OF THE COUNTRY AS THE KILLING OF A WHITE MOTHER'S SON, WE WHO BELIEVE IN FREEDOM CANNOT REST UNTIL THIS HAPPENS."

helping to found SNCC (pronounced "snick"), Ella showed young people that they had the power to improve their own lives.

Under Ella's guidance, SNCC recruited college students from all backgrounds: male and female, black and white, rich and poor. SNCC joined forces with another civil rights group, the Congress of Racial Equality (CORE). Together, they rode buses from state to state throughout the South. The "Freedom Riders" challenged segregation laws by peacefully occupying "white-only" areas in bus stations, restaurants, lunch counters, and restrooms. The Freedom Riders met **mob violence** with nonviolence and courage. Their bravery and determination caught the attention of Americans across the nation.

In the meantime, their mentor and teacher stayed in the background. "You didn't see me on television," Ella told an interviewer in 1977. "You didn't see news stories about me. My theory is strong people don't need strong leaders."

While her name is not well known, Ella was an **indispensable** person to the civil rights movement.

She listened to people. She cared about what they cared about. She taught them to work together. She made them believe that they could control their own destiny.

She recruited hundreds of ordinary people to join the NAACP and improve their own lives. In a movement that had few women leaders, Ella became the executive director of SCLC.

Ella was instrumental in founding SNCC, channeling the energy and hopes of a new generation of activists. As that generation matured, they continued to seek out Ella for her praise, criticism, advice, and wisdom.

Ella reminds us that it takes tireless workers behind the scenes to accomplish big things. Today, we can thank Ella for showing us how much good you can accomplish if you don't care who gets the credit.

EXPLORE MORE! Listen! A singing group called Sweet Honey in the Rock turned the Ella Baker quote featured here into a song called "Ella's Song."

DID YOU KNOW? The Ella Baker Center for Human Rights, located in Oakland, California, was founded in 1996. Building on the legacy of the civil rights icon, the center works to make communities safe, support the green jobs movement, ensure juvenile justice, and end police **brutality**.

VOTE
INTEGRATED SCHOOLS NOW!
FREEDOM

Medgar EVERS

{ 1925–1963 }

Medgar Evers once said that he just wanted to be an ordinary citizen. But Medgar was born in a time and a place that wouldn't let him be ordinary. Instead, he got involved in the civil rights movement and, by giving his life in the pursuit of civil rights, became the movement's first **martyr**.

Medgar was born and raised in Decatur, Mississippi. He had an older brother and two sisters. His family lived on a small farm where they raised a few animals. In addition to running their farm, Medgar's father worked at a **sawmill** and his mother did housekeeping.

Medgar's elementary school was a one-room shack with a leaky roof. One hundred black students, in grades one through eight, crowded into the shack to be taught by two overworked, dedicated teachers.

When Medgar was about fourteen years old, a family friend, Willie Tingle, was **lynched**. An angry group of white people dragged him through the streets behind a wagon and then killed him. The angry mob claimed that Willie had insulted a white woman.

No one was arrested for Willie's murder. Lynching was not a crime in Mississippi at that time. The incident made Medgar fearful for his own father's life. James Evers was a proud man who stood up for his rights. He refused to step off the sidewalk to let white people pass. He argued with white store owners who tried to cheat him. While Medgar was proud of his father, he worried that, one day, his father might meet the same fate as Willie Tingle.

During World War II, in 1943, Medgar dropped out of high school. He and his brother, Charles, enlisted in the U.S. Army. Medgar served in England and France. Medgar's experience in those two countries changed the course of his life.

While in France, Medgar saw that black and white Americans were treated equally by the French people. Medgar vowed that he would fight for change at home, too. After the war ended, Medgar and Charles returned to Mississippi to find that things had not changed. When the brothers went to vote, they were met by white men with guns who blocked their way. The brothers left without voting. At that time, black people were constantly being attacked for trying to exercise their right to vote.

Medgar finished high school and, in 1948, enrolled at Alcorn College. At the all-black school, Medgar studied business administration and was active in sports and school **politics**. He also met and married Myrlie Beasley. Medgar graduated in 1952.

The couple moved to Mound Bayou, Mississippi, a town developed by African Americans. Medgar became a traveling salesman. As he drove all over the state, Medgar witnessed extreme poverty and misery among his black customers. He renewed his vow to fight against racism.

Medgar became officially involved in the civil rights movement when he joined a local organization, the Regional Council of Negro Leadership (RCNL). He helped the RCNL organize a boycott of gasoline stations that wouldn't let black people use the stations' restrooms. The RCNL gave Medgar important experience and training that he would use later in his career.

In 1954, Medgar's father and role model passed away, and Medgar decided to become a lawyer. He applied to the all-white University of Mississippi Law School. The U.S. Supreme Court had recently ruled that public schools and colleges must be desegregated.

When the University of Mississippi rejected his application, Medgar went to the National Association for the Advancement of Colored People (NAACP) for advice. At that time, the NAACP was the best-known civil rights organization. The representative who spoke to Medgar was so impressed with the young man's determination that he offered Medgar a job. Medgar became the first field secretary for the NAACP in Mississippi.

As field secretary, Medgar worked to improve the lives of black Mississippians. He organized boycotts

"I LOVE MY CHILDREN AND I LOVE MY WIFE WITH ALL MY HEART. AND I WOULD DIE, DIE GLADLY, IF THAT WOULD MAKE A BETTER LIFE FOR THEM."

and started new chapters of the NAACP. He helped organize "wade-ins," which were protests against segregation at public beaches. Medgar called for boycotts to help integrate the city of Jackson's buses, public parks, and schools. He registered black people to vote. Medgar even investigated crimes, including the lynching of fourteen-year-old Emmett Till, an African American who had been visiting Mississippi from Chicago when he was murdered. One of Medgar's most well-known accomplishments was helping James Meredith (page 33) integrate the University of Mississippi, the college that had rejected Medgar seven years earlier.

As the fight for civil rights continued, Medgar Evers became the most famous civil rights leader in Mississippi. But Medgar's work also meant he was a target of white racists. He and his family lived in constant fear for their safety. On June 12, 1963, his family's worst fear came true. As Medgar arrived home from an NAACP meeting, he was shot to death.

On the night Medgar Evers was **assassinated**, his family had been watching President John F. Kennedy give a historic speech to the nation. The president had declared that the battle for civil rights was not just a legal fight but a **moral** one. Medgar once said, "You can kill a man, but you can't kill an idea." And the idea that Medgar died for—that all Americans are equal—lives on today.

Medgar was buried in Arlington National Cemetery, a burial place for those who have fought in the country's wars. Medgar had fought in two wars: in World War II and at home, in the civil rights movement.

Though his life was cut short, Medgar Evers was able to make a difference for black people in his home state of Mississippi. He helped desegregate schools, businesses, and parks. He investigated crimes against black people. He showed black Mississippians how to fight for their rights.

EXPLORE MORE! Get to know Myrlie Evers-Williams, the widow of Medgar Evers. She is a civil rights activist in her own right. In the book *For Us, the Living* by William Peters, she tells her story.

DID YOU KNOW? *USNS Medgar Evers* is a U.S. Navy cargo ship named in honor of World War II veteran and civil rights hero Medgar Evers. Launched in 2011, *USNS Medgar Evers* helps transfer supplies to other U.S. Navy ships.

UNIVERSIT
ISSISSIPP

James MEREDITH

{ 1933–Present }

James Howard Meredith's first experience with racial discrimination happened during a train trip from Chicago, Illinois, to the South. When the train arrived in Memphis, Tennessee, fifteen-year-old James was ordered to move to the black section, which was very crowded. He had to stand for the rest of the way home. James vowed that he would dedicate his life to fighting for equal treatment for African Americans.

James was raised with nine sisters and brothers on an 80-acre farm in **rural** Mississippi. The family grew cotton, corn, and other food crops. They were so poor that they did not have running water. But as far as James's father, Moses Meredith, was concerned, they had everything they needed. James's parents strongly believed in being independent.

Moses and Roxie Meredith were also passionate about education. They made sure that all 10 of their children graduated from high school. Seven, including James, went on to college. That was an enormous accomplishment for a poor black family living in Mississippi in the 1940s.

When James's father was around white people, he refused to act like a **second-class citizen**, as was expected of Southern black people. Moses taught his children that they were never to enter the home of a white family through the back door. They were never to work in service to whites: not as cooks or babysitters or maids. Taking his father's words to heart, James felt he had a "divine responsibility" to fight for equal rights.

After graduating from high school in 1951, James joined the newly integrated U.S. Air Force, serving as a clerk typist. In 1960, he left the military and prepared to study law by taking classes at several colleges. While engaged in his studies, James decided that he would embark upon three missions.

In 1961, James applied to the University of Mississippi ("Ole Miss"). Even though the U.S. Supreme Court had ordered that all public schools be desegregated, this university still admitted only white students. James's first mission was to force Ole Miss to obey the law.

When his application was rejected, James turned to the National Association for the Advancement of Colored People (NAACP) for help. The field secretary for the NAACP, Medgar Evers (page 27), filed a lawsuit against the school. The lawsuit claimed that the institution had rejected James because he was African American.

"I WAS ENGAGED IN A WAR. I CONSIDERED MYSELF ENGAGED IN A WAR FROM DAY ONE. AND MY OBJECTIVE WAS TO FORCE THE FEDERAL GOVERNMENT—THE KENNEDY ADMINISTRATION AT THAT TIME—INTO A POSITION WHERE THEY WOULD HAVE TO USE THE UNITED STATES MILITARY FORCE TO ENFORCE MY RIGHTS AS A CITIZEN."

The lawsuit made its way to the highest court in the country. The Supreme Court ruled in James's favor. However, the governor of Mississippi declared that no school in Mississippi would be integrated while he was in office. On September 20, 1962, when James arrived at the campus, he found that the school's entrance was blocked.

Ten days later, James went to the school again. This time, President John F. Kennedy had sent 500 U.S. marshals to walk James safely to his dormitory on the campus. One hour after James was safely in his room, riots broke out. Segregationists gathered on the campus and fought with the federal agents. Cars were set on fire. Many of the school's buildings were damaged, and two people were killed.

Nonetheless, on October 1, 1962, James became the first black student to attend the University of Mississippi. James endured insults and threats and needed constant protection from U.S. marshals while on campus. But he studied hard and graduated on August 18, 1963.

James continued his education at the University of Ibadan in the African country of Nigeria. There, he earned a degree in economics. Now, James was ready for his second mission: a "March Against Fear."

In 1966, James planned to march 220 miles, from Memphis, Tennessee, to Jackson, Mississippi. He had two goals. He wanted to bring attention to the continuing racism in the South, and he wanted to encourage black people to vote after the passage of the Voting Rights Act of 1965. This act outlawed imposing a voting "tax" on black people. It also banned giving literacy tests to black citizens before they were allowed to vote.

James did not seek the involvement of major civil rights organizations. He walked alone or with any ordinary citizens who dared to join him. On the second day of his march, at the 26th mile, James was shot by a white man and suffered many wounds. He was rushed to the hospital. Fortunately, he survived. While James was recovering, people came from across the country and continued the march. Martin Luther King Jr. (page 61), Fannie Lou Hamer (page 49), and other well-known civil rights leaders joined the march.

The marchers faced death threats, arrests, and tear gas. James was able to rejoin the march toward the end. When he and other leaders entered Jackson, Mississippi, on June 26, 1966, they were leading about 15,000 marchers. It was the largest civil rights march in Mississippi's history. During the three-week march, more than 4,000 African Americans registered to vote.

On what he considers his third mission, James has continued to fight for civil rights. He has focused on educational inequalities that African Americans continue to face, especially in Mississippi. Part of his mission is to heal racial divisions. He has said that this can be done with honest dialogue—by simply talking to one another. To help with this third mission, James wrote a book called *A Mission from God: A Memoir and Challenge for America*.

James was one of several people directly responsible for desegregating the University of Mississippi. Today, all public educational institutions in the United States are open to every citizen. His work also brought many people to the polls to vote in important local and national elections. Now when the black students at the University of Mississippi walk past a life-size statue of James Meredith, they are reminded that he was brave enough to be the first and pave the way for them.

EXPLORE MORE! Learn more about James Meredith. Read the book *March On Children!: The Story of James Meredith's March Against Fear* by Katina Rankin.

DID YOU KNOW? The Voting Rights Act of 1965, signed into law by President Lyndon B. Johnson, aimed to overcome barriers that prevented African Americans from exercising their right to vote as guaranteed under the 15th Amendment to the U.S. Constitution. The Voting Rights Act is considered one of the most important pieces of civil rights legislation.

END SEGREGATION
ACROSS THE
CORE

James FARMER

{ 1920–1999 }

When James Farmer entered Howard University, he planned to become a minister. But before he graduated, he changed his mind. His father asked him what he was going to do. James answered, "Destroy segregation." For his entire career, James worked hard to do just that.

James was born in Marshall, Texas. His father, the son of former enslaved people, was a college professor. His mother was a former teacher. Surrounded by books and thoughtful conversation, James learned to read, write, and count at an early age. He started first grade when he was just four years old.

Also as a four-year-old, James learned a lesson about segregation. One day, while in town with his mother, James asked her to buy him a soda. His mother told him that he had to wait until they got home. The soda shop was for white people only. That was James's first encounter with racism.

"I WOULD LIKE FOR IT TO BE KNOWN THAT I FOUNDED THE CONGRESS OF RACIAL EQUALITY IN 1942, ORGANIZED THE FREEDOM RIDES IN 1961, AND ATTEMPTED TO BRING GANDHIAN TECHNIQUES OF NONVIOLENCE TO THE STRUGGLE FOR RACIAL EQUALITY IN THIS COUNTRY."

When James was ten, he went to the train station with his father to buy a ticket home for his uncle Fred, who had been visiting from New York. James listened as his father made up a story about an "emergency" to convince the station manager to sell him a ticket for a car with a bed. Normally, sleeping cars were reserved for white people only. His father, who was a minister as well as a professor, later explained, "I had to tell that lie about your uncle Fred. The Lord will forgive me." Still unhappy, James promised himself that he would find a way to end segregation. Black people should not have to lie to be treated as equal citizens.

In the meantime, James excelled in school. He skipped grades and graduated from high school in 1934 at the age of fourteen. He earned a scholarship to all-black Wiley College in Marshall, Texas.

James was an outstanding student. With his logic and **eloquence**, he was a star member of the debate team. His ability to persuade judges and audiences to see things his way would come in handy one day.

After graduating from Wiley College, James enrolled at Howard University's School of Religion. He planned to become a minister like his father. However, James was disappointed when he saw that his religion, like many others, practiced segregation.

While at Howard, James was introduced to the teachings of Mohandas Gandhi. A native of India, Gandhi was a lawyer who taught the people of India to protest peacefully. Because India was ruled by the British, Indians were treated as second-class citizens in their own country. Gandhi used sit-ins, boycotts, and marches to bring about change. James was convinced that those same nonviolent methods could work in the United States in the fight against racial injustice.

James graduated from Howard in 1941, the year the United States entered World War II. James had changed his mind about becoming a minister, but he had become a **pacifist**—someone who is opposed to war and violence. He refused to fight in World War II.

James moved to Chicago, Illinois, and joined a pacifist organization called **Fellowship** of **Reconciliation** (FOR). As a member of FOR, James gave anti-war speeches and, for the first time, used one of Gandhi's peaceful techniques. He led a successful sit-in to desegregate a popular Chicago restaurant.

With members of FOR, James co-founded another group they called the Congress of Racial Equality (CORE).

That group followed the Gandhian principles of nonviolent direct action to fight racial discrimination. CORE believed that racial injustice should be important to everyone and welcomed people of all races to join. Within a few years, CORE had more than 60,000 members across the country.

In the 1940s and 1950s, with little national attention, CORE worked to integrate neighborhoods, banks, amusement parks, and barbershops. By the 1960s, CORE had grown to 82,000 members. Still, James believed that without more publicity, CORE's actions were like "a flea gnawing on the ear of an elephant." They needed to do more to be noticed and draw attention to racial injustice.

In February 1961, James was chosen to be the national director of CORE. The organization partnered with the Student Nonviolent Coordinating Committee (SNCC) and organized the Freedom Rides. The goal of the Freedom Riders was to draw attention to segregated bus stations in the South. James, along with other black and white activists, rode buses from Washington, D.C., to New Orleans, Louisiana. Along the way, they faced repeated violence; at one point, their bus was firebombed. Some riders, including James, spent time in jail.

The Freedom Riders gained national attention. Many people who saw their peaceful protests on the evening news were learning for the first time about segregation laws in the South. As the director of CORE, James became known as one of the Big Six civil rights leaders, along with Martin Luther King Jr. (page 61); Roy Wilkins of the National Association for the Advancement of Colored People; Whitney Young, the head of the National Urban League; John Lewis of SNCC (page 67); and Dorothy Height (page 79) of the National Council of Negro Women. These six leaders worked together to coordinate their activities.

James described the Freedom Rides as his proudest achievement. The nonviolent tactics that CORE pioneered helped end segregation laws in the South. In 1998, James received the Presidential Medal of Freedom, the nation's highest civilian honor.

Brave people like James risked their lives to challenge segregation laws. Despite their commitment to nonviolence, James and his fellow protestors were met with violence wherever they went. James and CORE proved that remaining calm in the face of hatred and brutality could be more effective than fighting violence with violence. It helped bring about the change James had wanted to see since he was a little boy. Today, in the United States, there are no laws that segregate people by race in public places.

EXPLORE MORE! Learn more about another one of the Big Six civil rights leaders, Roy Wilkins, through the book *Roy Wilkins: Leader of the NAACP* by Calvin Craig Miller.

DID YOU KNOW? In 1941, as a member of CORE, twenty-one-year-old James Farmer was among a group of young leaders invited to the White House to speak with President Franklin D. Roosevelt. The only black person among the invitees, James spoke with the president and First Lady Eleanor Roosevelt. James was honored that they answered his questions and listened to his ideas.

Fannie Lou HAMER

{ 1917–1977 }

Fannie Lou Hamer was a different kind of civil rights leader. She had not gone to college. She did not use elegant words or quote Mohandas Gandhi. Yet Fannie Lou's voice was powerful because she spoke from her own experience. She knew what it felt like to be "sick and tired of being sick and tired."

Born in Mississippi, Fannie Lou Townsend was the youngest of the 20 children of Ella and James Townsend. The Townsends worked as sharecroppers on the plantation of W. D. Marlow in Sunflower County, Mississippi. At harvest time, sharecroppers turned over their crops to the owner, and in return, the sharecroppers were paid a small amount of money.

Fannie's childhood was filled with poverty, sickness, hard work, and brutality. From the age of six, Fannie picked cotton with her family. When she was only eight, Fanny witnessed a lynching—the murder of a black man by an angry white mob. The one bright spot of Fannie's childhood was the one-room school provided for the sharecroppers' children. Fannie was allowed to attend school when she wasn't needed in the fields. She loved reading, spelling bees, and reciting poetry. Unfortunately, Fannie had to leave school when she was twelve years old to help take care of her sick parents.

Fannie suffered from an illness called polio, which caused stiffness in her legs. Still, she worked alongside men and women in the cotton fields six days a week. By age thirteen, she could pick 300 pounds of cotton a day. For this exhausting work, Fannie earned a penny a pound.

Fannie continued to improve her reading during Bible study at her church. When Fannie was twenty-seven years old, the plantation owner discovered she could read. He gave her a job as recordkeeper for the plantation.

In 1945, Fannie married Perry Hamer, a tractor driver on the plantation. It seemed that Fanny's life would be the ordinary life of a Mississippi sharecropper. However, in 1962, when she was forty-five years old, Fannie attended a meeting arranged by the Student Nonviolent Coordinating Committee (SNCC). At the meeting, black people were encouraged to register to vote. Up until that time, Fannie did not know that black people had a right to vote.

Soon after the meeting, on August 31, Fannie and 17 of her neighbors boarded a bus and headed to the local courthouse to register to vote. When they arrived, only Fannie and one other person in the group were allowed to fill out an application. The officials then gave the two a college-level literacy test. Both failed the test and were not allowed to register.

"I'M GONNA BE STANDING UP, I'M GONNA BE MOVING FORWARD, AND IF THEY SHOOT ME, I'M NOT GOING TO FALL BACK, I'M GOING TO FALL 5 FEET 4 INCHES FORWARD."

On the drive back home, the bus was stopped by police. The black bus driver was arrested for driving a bus that was "the wrong color." While the passengers were held on the bus, Fannie, in her booming voice, began to sing. One song, "This Little Light of Mine," would become Fannie's signature song.

When the owner of the plantation where Fannie lived and worked learned that she had tried to register to vote, he fired her from her job as recordkeeper. Over the next few months, Fannie was the target of racists who were angry that she had dared try to exercise her right to vote. Fannie and her husband had to stay with friends because people fired shots into their home at night.

Even though her life was now in danger, Fannie remained active in the civil rights movement. She became a field marshal for SNCC, working to register poor people—black and white—to vote. Even after she passed the literacy test on her third try, Fannie was forced to pay a tax before she was finally allowed to register to vote. This poll tax was designed to discourage black people from voting.

In 1963, Fanny and members of SNCC traveled by bus to a conference in Charleston, South Carolina. When they made a rest stop on the way home, a highway patrolman arrived and threatened the bus driver. When Fannie tried to talk to the officer, he arrested her. She was taken to jail, where she was beaten with a club. It took Fannie over a month to heal, and she never fully recovered from the beating.

In 1964, Fannie helped organize Freedom Summer, during which hundreds of college students, black and white, went to the South to help with voter registration. That same summer, Fannie spoke at the Democratic National Convention, a gathering of thousands of people who had come to listen to speeches and choose the person they wanted to run for president of the United States. Fannie's moving speech helped pass the Voting Rights Act of 1965.

Now a national figure, Fannie spoke across the country, raising money to help the people of Mississippi. She was committed to organizing "everyday" people in her community. With the help of Dorothy Height (page 79), president of the National Council of Negro Women, Fannie started programs to help people in her community improve their diets. Fannie also believed that African Americans needed economic power: the ability to buy, sell, and produce their own goods.

Fannie started what she called a Pig Bank. She bought 35 female and 5 male pigs. Pregnant females were loaned to local families. They could keep the piglets that were produced and return the mama pig to the bank. About 300 families benefited from this program. Fannie also established the Freedom Farm Cooperative to provide homes and food for poor families. In addition, she raised money to help build 200 low-cost houses in Mississippi.

Despite illness, police beatings, and death threats, Fannie did not see herself as a victim. She felt empowered to help those around her. She showed bravery and ingenuity in helping solve the problems she and people in her community faced. She constantly sought new solutions to old problems. She stood up to injustice and encouraged others to join the movement. Fannie used her powerful voice to tell her own story.

EXPLORE MORE! To learn more about Fannie Lou Hamer, read *Voice of Freedom: Fannie Lou Hamer* by Carole Boston Weatherford.

DID YOU KNOW? Sharecropping was just one step above slavery. Sharecroppers rented small pieces of land to grow crops. They paid their rent and expenses by selling the landowner a portion of their crops. The landowners often overcharged for rent and necessities and underpaid the sharecroppers for their crops. Many sharecroppers were never able to pay off their debts to the landowners.

Bayard RUSTIN

{ 1912–1987 }

Bayard Rustin earned the nickname "Mr. March-on-Washington" for good reason—he organized it. But that statement doesn't do justice to the importance of Bayard's contributions to the civil rights movement. He was introduced to activism at an early age, and he remained committed to civil rights and nonviolence throughout his life.

Bayard was born in West Chester, Pennsylvania, and brought up by his well-to-do grandparents. Janifer Rustin, a caterer, and Julia Rustin, a nurse, raised Bayard along with their 11 children.

Julia was a member of the local chapter of the National Association for the Advancement of Colored People (NAACP). Prominent leaders of the organization frequently visited the Rustin home. Even in states outside the South, such as Pennsylvania, white and black people were segregated, either by **custom** or by law. From listening in on conversations of the NAACP members, Bayard learned to stand up for his rights.

In high school, Bayard was a member of the track team. At a state-wide track meet, he refused to compete unless he and a fellow black student were allowed to stay in the same hotel as their white teammates. Bayard won that battle. However, when he attempted to desegregate his hometown's movie theater as a teenager, he was arrested for "disturbing the peace."

Bayard graduated from high school in 1932. He attended colleges in New York, Ohio, and Pennsylvania. In New York, Bayard divided his time between his two great interests—music and civil rights.

In 1939, Bayard sang in the chorus of *John Henry*, an all-black musical starring the famous actor, singer, and activist Paul Robeson. Bayard continued to sing in his tenor voice at demonstrations and even in jails, but it was his civil rights activities that took center stage in his life.

Like many activists at the time, Bayard embraced nonviolence and pacifism—the belief that any violence, including war, was wrong. He was active in the pacifist Society of Friends (the Quakers). He was also influenced by Mohandas Gandhi's philosophy of nonviolence.

Bayard joined another pacifist group, Fellowship of Reconciliation (FOR), and was elected to be its youth secretary. In 1942, he traveled throughout the nation, hoping to recruit more pacifists to protest against World War II. In his journeys, Bayard sought to desegregate bus travel between states. When he boarded a bus going from Louisville, Kentucky, to Nashville, Tennessee, the driver asked him to move to the back. Bayard refused. He was arrested

"WE NEED, IN EVERY COMMUNITY, A GROUP OF ANGELIC TROUBLEMAKERS."

and beaten. Years later, he explained that he protested because he thought that if white passengers never saw a black person protest the law, they would think black people liked sitting in the back.

In 1944, because he refused to sign up to fight in World War II, Bayard was sent to prison for more than two years. After his release in 1947, he joined the Congress of Racial Equality (CORE). Five years after his first attempt to desegregate buses, he participated in CORE's campaign to end segregation in interstate bus travel. This time, Bayard was dragged from the front of a bus by police and sentenced to 30 days on a chain gang, a group of prisoners chained together while working.

Despite the chain gang experience and the failure of the campaign, Bayard's belief in nonviolence was unshaken. The following year, he traveled to India to learn more about nonviolent resistance firsthand from leaders of the Gandhian movement. When he returned, he met Martin Luther King Jr. (page 61) and started working with him. King was in the middle of the Montgomery Bus Boycott in Alabama. Bayard advised King on the tactics of civil disobedience and taught him about Gandhi's philosophy of nonviolent resistance.

In 1962, Bayard was asked to help with the March on Washington for Jobs and Freedom. The march was being organized by the most prominent leaders of the civil rights movement. They wanted the march to be the largest demonstration ever held in the capital and to have extensive television coverage. The leaders knew Bayard had organizing experience, so they made him the chief coordinator. He was in charge of training off-duty police officers to control the crowds, showing bus drivers how to direct traffic, scheduling the speakers, and more.

The march, held in August 1963, was a huge success. More than 250,000 people attended. There were only four arrests. The march will always be remembered for King's stirring "I Have a Dream" speech. But those who were aware of all the work that went into planning the march knew that it would not have happened if not for Bayard.

The March on Washington helped bring about the Civil Rights Act of 1964, which prohibits discrimination on the basis of race, color, religion, sex, or national origin. It also led to the Voting Rights Act of 1965, which outlawed literacy tests and poll taxes meant to keep black people from voting.

The march was Bayard's crowning achievement. Bayard once wrote: "The principal factors which influenced my life are 1) nonviolent tactics; 2) constitutional means; 3) democratic procedures; 4) respect for human personality; 5) a belief that all people are one." Bayard employed all five principles in planning the March on Washington. It took all of the experiences, knowledge, and skills he had acquired over his remarkable life to produce it. But Bayard's work was not finished when the march ended. Later in life, he became an outspoken activist for the rights of gay people.

Bayard Rustin was awarded the Presidential Medal of Freedom in 2013, after his death. The medal recognizes people who have made "an especially meritorious contribution to the security or national interests of the United States."

EXPLORE MORE! Go online to hear Bayard Rustin sing a beautiful rendition of a song that speaks to the life he led, "Nobody Knows the Trouble I've Seen."

DID YOU KNOW? Mohandas Gandhi (1869–1948) was known to his many followers as "Mahatma," or "the great-souled one." He is considered one of the 20th century's greatest political and spiritual leaders. Honored in India as the father of the nation, he pioneered the principle of satyagraha—resistance to tyranny through nonviolent civil disobedience.

PROUD
LOVE

Martin Luther KING JR.

{ 1929–1968 }

On the night of April 3, 1968, Martin Luther King Jr. gave a remarkable speech. "We've got some difficult days ahead," he admitted. "But it really doesn't matter with me now [. . .] Like anybody, I would like to live a long life [. . .] But I'm not concerned about that now. I just want to do God's will." The civil rights leader was killed the next day.

Martin Luther King Jr. was born and raised in Atlanta, Georgia. His father was the pastor of Ebenezer Baptist Church. His mother, Alberta, was the church's choir director and organist. Martin, his sister, and his brother took piano lessons from their mother and enjoyed listening to their grandmother's Bible stories.

Martin's experience with Jim Crow was typical for an African American child growing up in the South during the 1930s. When he and a close playmate turned six, they went to separate schools. Martin went to one for black children and his playmate to one for white children. Soon, his playmate's parents told Martin he could no longer play with their son. As he grew up, Martin often saw his father rebel against Jim Crow laws.

In high school, Martin gave his first public speech during an oratorical contest. He stated, "Black America still wears chains." Martin won the contest. On the bus ride home, Martin was furious when he and his teacher were forced to give up their seats to white passengers.

Martin skipped the ninth and the twelfth grades and, at the age of fifteen, was admitted to Morehouse College in Atlanta. Like his father, grandfather, great-grandfather, and uncle before him, Martin planned to become a preacher. After graduating from Morehouse, Martin went on to study religion, first at Crozer Theological Seminary and then at Boston University. There, Martin was introduced to ideas about civil disobedience and Gandhi's methods of peaceful protest.

While studying at Boston, Martin met and married Coretta Scott. Martin graduated with a doctoral degree in theology, which earned him the title "Dr." He and Coretta moved to Montgomery, Alabama. There, Martin would begin his ministry as the pastor of the Dexter Avenue Baptist Church.

Less than a year after Martin and Coretta arrived in Montgomery, the city became the focus of the civil rights movement. On December 5, 1955, the new pastor, only twenty-six years old, was asked to lead a bus boycott. The protest had been called when Rosa Parks (page 7) was arrested for not giving up her seat to a white person on a

"I HAVE A DREAM THAT MY FOUR LITTLE CHILDREN WILL ONE DAY LIVE IN A NATION WHERE THEY WILL NOT BE JUDGED BY THE COLOR OF THEIR SKIN BUT BY THE CONTENT OF THEIR CHARACTER."

Montgomery city bus. For 385 days, Martin kept the boycotters' morale up with energizing speeches.

The boycott proved to be a dangerous time for Martin and his family. They received threatening phone calls and letters. Martin spent two weeks in jail. Worst of all, on the evening of January 30, 1956, a man tossed a bomb onto the porch of his house. Fortunately, even though his wife and their baby were at home, no one was hurt. News of the bombing spread quickly.

By the time Martin made it home to see if his wife and baby were okay, a crowd had gathered outside. They were angry about the bomb. A few minutes later, Martin stood on his damaged porch and addressed the crowd: "If you have weapons, take them home [. . .] We must meet violence with nonviolence [. . .] We must meet hate with love. Remember, if I am stopped, this movement will not stop."

The boycott ended on December 20, 1956. The U.S. Supreme Court had upheld a lower court ruling that banned racial segregation on all Montgomery public buses.

After the boycott, Martin and other black ministers formed the Southern Christian Leadership Conference (SCLC), with Martin as its president. SCLC's goal was to empower black churches to peacefully protest segregation and discrimination.

As president of SCLC, Martin kept a demanding schedule. He gave more than 2,500 speeches. He traveled over six million miles. He went to jail 29 times. In the meantime, his life was constantly being threatened. He survived a stabbing in 1958. Through it all, Martin maintained his belief in nonviolence. In his book *Why We Can't Wait*, Martin wrote: "In the nonviolent army, there is room for everyone who wants to join up. There is no color distinction. There is no examination, no pledge, except that [. . .] nonviolent soldiers are called upon to examine and burnish their greatest weapons: their heart, their conscience, their courage, and their sense of justice."

On August 28, 1963, Martin Luther King Jr. led 250,000 members of his "nonviolent army" on a march through the streets of Washington, D.C. This event was called the March on Washington for Jobs and Freedom. From the steps of the Lincoln Memorial, he made a 17-minute speech that was a lesson in history, geography, and economics. His words opened wounds and healed them at the same time. He talked about how far African Americans had come. He acknowledged how far they had to go. He gave them hope that they would get there. The most familiar part of the speech, in which Martin shared his dream of freedom, justice, and brotherhood, was unplanned.

Tragically, five years after his "I Have a Dream" speech, Martin was assassinated. But, in that one speech, Martin had summarized his beliefs and his mission. He left a map for going forward. Today, it still shows us the way to realize his dream. He believed that the way to achieve social justice and equality is through nonviolence, unity, and love.

During his short life, Martin made an enormous contribution to the cause of civil rights. He once said, "Greatness is determined by service." The honors he received are a testament to his service: the Congressional Gold Medal, the Presidential Medal of Freedom, the Nobel Peace Prize, a 30-foot-tall monument, and a national holiday.

EXPLORE MORE! You can learn more about Martin Luther King Jr. by visiting the King Center in Atlanta, Georgia, in person or online at TheKingCenter.org.

DID YOU KNOW? The Nobel Peace Prize is awarded to people who have benefited humankind. Martin Luther King Jr. received the prize for his leadership and commitment to nonviolent action. He accepted the award on December 10, 1964, and pledged the prize money of $54,600 to the civil rights movement's continued development. At the age of thirty-five, he was the youngest person to receive the award.

John LEWIS

{1940–2020}

If not for his family's large battery-powered radio, John Lewis might have followed his parents' advice to accept things the way they were. He might have become a preacher and stayed out of trouble. But, after hearing a powerful voice on the radio, John decided that it was his calling to make trouble—good trouble.

John was born in the all-black rural town of Troy, Alabama. He was the third of 10 children. His parents were sharecroppers. When John was four, his family moved to a 110-acre farm of their own. Their farmhouse had no running water, electricity, or heat.

John began his education at the two-room schoolhouse near his farm. Like his home, the school lacked running water and electricity. The students had two teachers, one for each of the two classrooms. They learned from textbooks thrown away by the local white schools.

When not in school, John worked on the family farm, picking peanuts, corn, and cotton. John was also in charge of taking care of the chickens. He fed them and read to

"THE WORLD I KNEW AS A LITTLE BOY WAS A RICH, HAPPY ONE [. . .] WE WERE POOR [. . .] BUT I DIDN'T REALIZE IT. IT WAS A SMALL WORLD, A SAFE WORLD, FILLED WITH FAMILY AND FRIENDS."

them from his Bible. His family called him "Preacher," and it seemed John was destined to become one.

Sometimes John and his siblings went into town to see movies at the theater. White children were seated on the lower level. Black children were escorted up an outside stairway and then back inside to the balcony to watch the movie. John remembered asking his parents why black and white children could not go to the same school or sit together in the theater. He also asked why black people could not check out books from the public library. John said his parents told him, "That's the way it is, don't get in trouble."

In 1955, on his family's radio, John heard the words of Dr. Martin Luther King Jr. (page 61). John learned that, 50 miles away, a brave bus rider named Rosa Parks (page 7) had refused to give up her seat to a white person. What he heard inspired him to protest against the injustices he saw. He decided he would make "good trouble, necessary trouble."

A short time later, sixteen-year-old John led his brothers, sisters, and cousins to their town's public library.

Each asked to apply for a library card. Each was told by the librarian that the library was for white people only. Not willing to give up, John gathered signatures for a **petition**, a written complaint. Although nothing came of the petition, John would continue to "make trouble."

In 1957, he became the first member of his family to graduate from high school. After graduation, he enrolled in the American Baptist Theological Seminary in Nashville, Tennessee. He planned to become a preacher. While at the seminary, John met many civil rights activists. He also continued to be moved by the speeches of Martin Luther King Jr. that he heard on the radio. John wrote him a letter, and in response, Dr. King sent John a bus ticket to come to Montgomery to meet with him.

That ticket led to John's formal entry into the civil rights movement. He began working with Dr. King, Rosa Parks, and other civil rights leaders. In 1961, John became one of the original 13 Freedom Riders, the black and white activists who challenged segregation by riding buses through the South. They stopped at stations and entered areas that were designated "whites only." John and the other Freedom Riders were beaten mercilessly and jailed. White Freedom Riders, such as John's lifelong friend Jim Zwerg, were treated as brutally as the black Freedom Riders.

John helped form the Student Nonviolent Coordinating Committee (SNCC), which organized lunch counter sit-ins. In 1963, as SNCC's leader, John was chosen to give a speech at the March on Washington. Speaking before

Dr. King, John declared, "We do not want to go to jail. But we will go to jail if this is the price we must pay for love, brotherhood, and true peace."

The defining event of John's career happened on March 7, 1965. He led a group of 600 people on a march across the Edmund Pettus Bridge in Selma, Alabama. The march was to demand that black people be allowed to exercise their right to vote. When the group was halfway across the bridge, state troopers ordered them to turn back and leave. The marchers refused. They stood silently and peacefully on the bridge. The troopers responded with vicious force. John and many of the protestors were beaten with clubs and whips. The day became known as "Bloody Sunday." Images on television of the troopers' brutality shocked viewers across the country. Americans demanded that black people be allowed to vote in peace. Not long after Bloody Sunday, President Lyndon B. Johnson signed the Voting Rights Act of 1965 into law.

After his days as an activist were over, John decided to work for change from within the government. In 1986, he was elected to Congress as a representative from Georgia. He served for 34 years. As a member of Congress, one of his goals was to make sure that the civil rights gains of the 1950s and 1960s were not forgotten. To that end, John was instrumental in establishing the National Museum of African American History and Culture. Now, for generations to come, the brave deeds of those who fought for the rights enjoyed today will be remembered.

John also wrote books about his experience on the front lines of the civil rights movement. On July 5, 1998, he went back to his hometown of Troy, Alabama, for a book signing at the public library. Black and white citizens showed up. After signing hundreds of copies of his autobiography, *Walking with the Wind*, John received quite a surprise. The librarian presented him with the item he had requested four decades earlier: a library card.

EXPLORE MORE! To learn more about the Freedom Riders, read *Freedom Riders: John Lewis and Jim Zwerg on the Front Lines of the Civil Rights Movement* by Ann Bausum.

DID YOU KNOW? The National Museum of African American History and Culture is the only national museum devoted exclusively to the documentation of African American life, history, and culture. It opened its doors in 2016 as the newest museum of the Smithsonian Institution. Located in Washington, D.C., the museum may be visited in person or online at NMAAHC.si.edu.

Malcolm X

{ 1925–1965 }

Malcolm X went from an angry young man involved in criminal activities to one of the most influential leaders in the fight for equal rights. He urged black Americans to learn about their history and to be proud of their African heritage and culture. He believed that they must fight for their rights "by any means necessary."

Malcolm Little was born in Omaha, Nebraska, the fourth child of Earl and Louise Little. Malcolm's parents were active in the Universal Negro Improvement Association (UNIA), which believed in creating a separate nation for black people. His father, a Baptist preacher, was constantly harassed by the Ku Klux Klan. They considered Earl a "troublemaker."

The family moved often. One of their homes was destroyed in a suspicious fire. But the death threats did not stop. In 1931, when Malcolm was six, his father died in what police called a streetcar accident. However, his family and friends believed he was murdered by the Ku Klux Klan. The family was left in poverty. Malcolm's mother never got over the shock and grief of her husband's death. In 1938, she was declared mentally ill and committed to a hospital. Her children were separated, and Malcolm ended up in foster care.

While in foster care, Malcolm attended a mostly white junior high school. A good student, Malcolm shared with a teacher that he had hopes of becoming a lawyer. The teacher told Malcolm that being a lawyer was not a realistic goal for a black child. Disheartened, fifteen-year-old Malcolm dropped out of school and went to live with his half-sister in Boston.

In Boston, Malcolm held a variety of jobs. Later he moved to New York City, where he worked for the railroad but also got involved in crime. In late 1945, Malcolm returned to Boston. He broke into people's homes, stealing jewelry and other valuables. In 1946, at the age of twenty-one, full of anger and resentment, Malcolm began serving an eight- to ten-year sentence for burglary.

While in prison, Malcolm first heard the teachings of Elijah Muhammad, the head of the Nation of Islam, also called Black Muslims. The Nation of Islam taught that black people were better than white people. Black Muslims believed that black people should have a separate nation for themselves within the United States. The group taught its members self-reliance, self-respect, and pride in their African heritage.

The message of the Nation of Islam appealed to Malcolm. He began signing his name "Malcolm X." He explained, "For me, my 'X' replaced the white slave

"MY ALMA MATER WAS BOOKS, A GOOD LIBRARY . . . I COULD SPEND THE REST OF MY LIFE READING, JUST SATISFYING MY CURIOSITY."

master name of 'Little.'" In late 1948, Malcolm wrote to Muhammad. The leader of the Nation of Islam advised Malcolm to let go of his past, humbly bow in prayer to Allah (God), and promise never to engage in crime or destructive behavior again.

Malcolm agreed and became a Black Muslim. After serving six years, Malcolm was released from prison. He was made a minister and the head of the Harlem mosque (place of worship) of the Nation of Islam. Malcolm's sermons attracted many new followers. Membership in the Nation of Islam climbed from 500 in 1952 to 30,000 in 1963. People outside the Nation of Islam began coming to hear Malcolm speak. He lectured around the country.

Like Martin Luther King Jr. (page 61), Malcolm was a powerful orator. However, their messages were very different. King believed that all people were equal. He insisted that black people could achieve their rights through peaceful means. Malcolm preached that black people could never live in peace with white people. He declared that black people should use "any means necessary" to gain their rights.

The Nation of Islam and **mainstream** civil rights leaders also disagreed about what rights they were fighting for. One of the goals of the civil rights movement was to register more black people to vote. Civil rights organizations believed that it was important for African Americans to have a say in their government. By contrast, the Nation of Islam did not allow its members to vote. Black Muslims were forbidden by their leaders to participate in politics at all.

Malcolm X believed in segregation, or separation of the two races. His message **resonated** with black people who felt anger and resentment over their struggles in the United States. Malcolm did not ask African Americans to love white people. He urged them to love themselves. Malcolm's message drew both anger and admiration from black people and white people.

Malcolm challenged black people to look at themselves differently. At a 1962 rally, Malcolm asked: "Who taught you to hate the color of your skin? [...] Who taught you to hate yourself from the top of your head to the soles of your feet? Who taught you to hate your own kind?"

Malcolm's message gave rise to books, movies, songs, television shows, clothing trends, and hairstyles that showed pride and self-respect. Malcolm popularized the phrases "Black Power" and "Black is Beautiful."

Eventually, Malcolm began to question some of the beliefs of the Nation of Islam. On March 8, 1964, he announced that he was leaving the group and creating a new organization that would be more involved in politics.

He also expressed a desire to work with other civil rights leaders.

In April 1964, Malcolm traveled to Mecca, Islam's holiest city. He saw, for the first time, Muslims of all colors worshipping together. He decided that white people were not the problem. Hate was the problem. Malcolm grew more optimistic that America's race problems could be solved peacefully.

Like other prominent civil rights leaders, Malcolm received countless death threats. On February 14, 1965, attackers firebombed Malcolm's New York house while he and his family were asleep inside. Fortunately, no one was hurt.

However, one week later, when he was thirty-nine years old, Malcolm was assassinated. His beliefs had gone through a profound change before he died. He had come to believe that violence was not the answer; hate was not the cure to what ailed the country. One of his beliefs remained constant and echoes today: Before you can love someone else, you must love yourself.

EXPLORE MORE! Read a graphic novel about Malcolm X by Gary Jeffrey, *Malcolm X and the Fight for African American Unity.*

DID YOU KNOW? Mecca is the holiest city in Islam and a city in Saudi Arabia. Mecca, which only Muslims are allowed to visit, is the birthplace of the Islamic prophet Muhammad and of the faith itself.

NCNW

Dorothy HEIGHT

{ 1912–2010 }

To Dorothy Height, achieving civil rights meant more than black people being treated the same as white people. It also meant women having the same rights as men. It meant black people being able to find jobs, learn how to read, and vote. Throughout her long life, Dorothy Height worked tirelessly to help people accomplish these goals.

Dorothy was born in Richmond, Virginia. She was the daughter of James Height, a builder and painter, and Fannie Height, a nurse. When she was about five, Dorothy's family moved to Pittsburgh, Pennsylvania. There, Dorothy went to school with children of all races.

Dorothy remembered experiencing very little prejudice growing up. Still, Dorothy began her lifelong fight for civil rights as a teenager. She became active in anti-lynching campaigns. In the 1920s, lynchings—the brutal killing of black people by white mobs—usually went unpunished. Anti-lynching groups tried to get laws passed to make lynching a crime. By marching and speaking out publicly, these groups also made more people across the country aware of lynchings.

After graduating from high school with honors in 1929, Dorothy had a personal experience with racism. She was accepted at Barnard College in New York, a well-known college for women. But when she arrived to enroll, the college dean told Dorothy that Barnard had already reached its limit of "two Negro students per year." Dorothy was so upset that she could not sleep or eat for days. But soon, she was ready to "go into action." Her rejection taught her that there was no advantage in being bitter. Instead, it increased her "determination to eliminate discrimination."

Dorothy applied to New York University (NYU), where she was readily accepted. After graduating from NYU, she attended Columbia University and then the New York School of Social Work.

In 1934, Dorothy began working in New York City as a social worker, helping people and families in need. During her time as a social worker, she developed skills as a peacemaker. She would go on to spend much of her career settling arguments and solving problems that arose when people with different ideas worked together.

After about three years, Dorothy became a counselor for the Young Women's Christian Association (YWCA) of New York. In 1937, at a YWCA event, Dorothy met Mary McLeod Bethune, a famous educator and civil rights leader. At the same event, Dorothy was introduced to Eleanor Roosevelt, the beloved First Lady of the

"FOR THE REST OF MY LIFE, I WILL BE WORKING FOR EQUALITY, FOR JUSTICE, TO ELIMINATE RACISM, TO BUILD A BETTER LIFE FOR OUR FAMILIES AND OUR CHILDREN."

United States. Dorothy would go on to work with these two women for many years on their common goal of increasing educational opportunities and equal rights for black people and women.

McLeod Bethune was the founder and president of the National Council of Negro Women (NCNW). Its mission was to improve opportunities for black women in politics and education. She convinced Dorothy to join the council, saying, "The Freedom Gates are half ajar. We must pry them fully open."

When Dorothy first began working for the YWCA, black people in some states were not allowed to swim in the pools at YWCA chapters. In 1946, Dorothy was elected as the national interracial education secretary of the YWCA. In that position, she made sure that people of all races were allowed to use the facilities in every YWCA chapter.

In 1957, Dorothy was elected president of the NCNW. As a leader of both the YWCA and the NCNW, Dorothy's influence reached far beyond those organizations. Presidents Dwight D. Eisenhower and Lyndon B. Johnson often asked Dorothy for advice. She encouraged President

Eisenhower to end segregation in public schools. She also urged President Johnson to appoint black women to government positions.

Dorothy was the only woman among the "Civil Rights Big Six." These were people who, through the organizations they headed, were considered the leaders of the civil rights movement. Besides Dorothy, the group included Martin Luther King Jr. (page 61), James Farmer (page 41), John Lewis (page 67), Roy Wilkins, and Whitney Young.

In 1963, Dorothy served as one of the chief organizers of the March on Washington for Jobs and Freedom. She worked closely with Bayard Rustin (page 55) on the complex planning involved. She raised money and offered the NCNW headquarters in Washington for planning meetings. Dorothy also resolved conflicts that arose among the organizers of the march. As the representative for the NCNW, Dorothy was the only woman on the stage when Dr. King gave his "I Have a Dream" speech.

Dorothy retired from the YWCA in 1977 when she was sixty-five years old. At age eighty-five, she retired from the NCNW. However, Dorothy remained active in civil rights until she was in her nineties. Today the YWCA and the NCNW continue the work to which Dorothy devoted her life.

Dorothy worked for change. And, unlike many in the civil rights movement, she saw considerable change during her lifetime. To her, it was important not to be bitter and to recognize progress when it happened.

For Dorothy, some of the changes were simple and personal. Seventy-five years after it rejected her because of her skin color, Barnard College made her an honorary alumna (graduate). She also got to see the country elect the first African American president. Speaking of Barack Obama's election, Dorothy remarked, "I believed that it would come [. . .] I'm so glad I lived to see it."

EXPLORE MORE! Dorothy Height dedicated her life to the YWCA. Visit the YWCA's website, YWCA.org, and learn about this organization's history, its evolving mission, and the many services it offers to women, girls, and families today.

DID YOU KNOW? Dorothy Height found a friend and mentor in Mary McLeod Bethune (1875–1955). The daughter of formerly enslaved people, she was one of the most important leaders in education, civil rights, and women's rights during the 20th century. The college she founded set educational standards for today's black colleges, and her role as an advisor to President Franklin D. Roosevelt gave African Americans a voice in government.

Anna Pauline "Pauli" MURRAY

{ 1910–1985 }

Anna Pauline "Pauli" Murray played an essential role in the civil rights movement. She worked behind the scenes, writing important books, papers, and documents that were used to fight discrimination. She helped Thurgood Marshall (page 13) win the *Brown v. Board of Education* Supreme Court case. And Pauli was there demanding that the male civil rights leaders allow women's voices to be heard.

Pauli was born in Baltimore, Maryland, and raised in North Carolina by her grandparents. Pauli had African, European, and Indigenous ancestry. She came from people who were enslaved and from slave owners. However, both of Pauli's parents identified as black.

Her mother died when Pauli was three, and her father was too ill to take care of his six children. Pauli was sent to Durham, North Carolina, to live with her grandparents and aunts. She thrived in her new home. She was a curious, energetic, and intelligent child. She taught herself to read by the age of five. She attended the Episcopal church with her family. By the time she was fifteen, Pauli was the editor-in-chief of the school newspaper, the president of the literary society, class secretary, a member of the debate club, and a forward on the basketball team.

From the moment Pauli learned about Jim Crow laws, she actively resisted them. She walked everywhere so she would not have to ride on segregated buses. She boycotted the movie theater rather than sit in the balcony. From the time she was ten years old, Pauli talked about moving to the North and escaping Jim Crow.

When she was sixteen, Pauli was finally allowed to leave Durham because her all-black high school only went to the eleventh grade. Pauli moved to New York, where she lived with a cousin's family. She enrolled in Richmond Hill High School, where she was the only African American out of 4,000 students. Pauli graduated with honors in 1927.

When Pauli applied to college, she was met with both racism and sexism. About this time, Pauli started going by her middle name, which she shortened from Pauline to Pauli. She did not want people to know from her name if she was male or female. Her first choice for college was Columbia University, but the school did not admit women, so, in 1928, she enrolled at Hunter College, a free city university. Planning to become a writer, Pauli graduated in 1933 with a bachelor's degree in English.

After working at a variety of jobs, she applied to the University of North Carolina. It rejected her because of her race, even though two of Pauli's white ancestors had

"IT HAS TAKEN ME ALMOST A LIFETIME TO DISCOVER THAT TRUE EMANCIPATION LIES IN THE ACCEPTANCE OF THE WHOLE PAST, IN DERIVING STRENGTH FROM ALL MY ROOTS, IN FACING UP TO THE DEGRADATION AS WELL AS THE DIGNITY OF MY ANCESTORS."

attended the university. Not long after that disappointment, Pauli and a companion were asked to move to the back of a bus while riding through Virginia. They refused. The driver called the police. The two women spent several days in jail. Pauli vowed she would never return to Virginia. However, she found herself in the state again after being asked to give a speech on behalf of a sharecropper who had been wrongly accused of murdering the landowner for whom he worked.

Pauli's powerful speech was attended by lawyers Thurgood Marshall and Leon Ransom. The two men were so impressed by Pauli's speech that they suggested she apply to the Howard University Law School. Pauli enrolled at Howard with "the single-minded intention of destroying Jim Crow."

At Howard, Pauli experienced sexism from fellow students and faculty. She made up the term "Jane Crow" to describe the kind of discrimination women faced. When one of her professors announced to his class that he didn't know why a woman would want to go to law school, Pauli vowed that she would be number one in her class. True to her word, she graduated as valedictorian in 1944.

Pauli's graduation paper was an argument against the 1896 Supreme Court case *Plessy v. Ferguson*, which allowed segregation in public places. Pauli's paper would be used 10 years later by Thurgood Marshall to successfully argue that segregation in public schools was unconstitutional.

In 1960, when Pauli returned from an overseas job, the civil rights movement was at its height. The women's movement, however, was just beginning. In 1963, Pauli criticized civil rights leaders for not inviting any women to speak at the March on Washington. Pauli came to believe that women needed their own civil rights organization. Two years after the March on Washington, Pauli joined famous **feminist** Betty Friedan and others in founding the National Organization for Women. Its goal was to achieve and protect equal rights for all women.

In the meantime, Pauli became the first African American to receive a doctorate in judicial (legal) science from Yale Law School. Pauli was hired as a professor at Brandeis University, where she taught law, African American studies, and women's studies.

In 1977, Pauli became the first African American woman to become an Episcopal priest. She wrote: "Now I was empowered to minister the sacrament of One in whom there is no north or south, no black or white, no male or female—only the spirit of love and reconciliation drawing us all toward the goal of human wholeness."

Pauli played many roles in her life: activist, lawyer, poet, writer, priest. Her legal writings, speeches, and books helped create the laws we live by today. They still provide tools and strategies for those continuing her fight against injustice.

Pauli fought for equality for black people *and* for women of all colors. She fought for a number of social justice causes. But every fight was a reflection of her singular passion—to help humankind live in a kinder and more just way.

EXPLORE MORE! You can visit the Pauli Murray Center for History and Social Justice in person or online at PauliMurrayCenter.com. The center's main building is Pauli's Durham, North Carolina, childhood home.

DID YOU KNOW? Pauli Murray wrote an argument that Thurgood Marshall used to overturn *Plessy v. Ferguson.* This was an 1896 Supreme Court decision that ruled that segregation was legal, as long as equal facilities were provided for black and white people.

BLACK
PANTHER
PARTY

Robert "Bobby" SEALE

{ 1936–Present }

Robert "Bobby" Seale was a civil rights activist who insisted that black neighborhoods needed to be served and protected by any means necessary. He believed that black men and women should be free to exercise their right to vote. He also believed their children deserved a good education and a healthy breakfast.

Bobby was born in Liberty, Texas, and was the oldest of three children. His parents were George Seale, a carpenter, and Thelma Seale, a homemaker. The family lived in poverty during most of Bobby's early life. They left Texas and moved to Oakland, California, when Bobby was eight.

Bobby and his siblings attended public schools. At Berkeley High School, Bobby tried out for the basketball and football teams. When he failed to make either team, he blamed it on racial prejudice. Frustrated, Bobby dropped out of school. In 1955, he joined the U.S. Air Force.

Three years later, he was released from the air force after he was found guilty of fighting with a commanding officer. Bobby returned to Oakland and worked as a mechanic while studying for his high school diploma at night. In 1960, after earning his diploma, he attended Merritt Community College, where he studied engineering and politics. Bobby joined the Afro-American Association (AAA), a group that believed in **black separatism**, or black people living separately from white people. Bobby met a fellow member of the AAA named Huey Newton. The two quickly became friends.

Bobby and Newton grew dissatisfied with the AAA. The group seemed more interested in discussing black culture than in defeating racism. Bobby and Newton wanted to fight against racial injustice. They were inspired by the powerful teachings of Malcolm X (page 73). Bobby had heard him speak in Oakland.

In October 1966, Bobby and Newton co-founded the Black Panther Party for Self-Defense (BPP). Bobby served as the chairman and Newton as the minister of defense. The BPP rejected the nonviolent approach of the more popular civil rights leaders. The BPP adopted Malcolm X's slogan "Freedom by any means necessary." The BPP founders created a document called the "Ten-Point Program." It listed items that the BPP demanded from the federal government on behalf of black people. Among them were land, food, housing, education, justice, and peace.

An important part of the BPP's mission was their "Policing the Police" program. The purpose of the program was to end police brutality in Oakland. To do this, Black

"ELECTORAL POLITICS WAS ALWAYS AN OBJECTIVE OF THE BLACK PANTHER PARTY, SO BARACK OBAMA IS A PART OF WHAT WE DREAMED AND STRUGGLED AND DIED FOR."

Panthers showed up, armed with guns, wearing black berets (hats) and leather jackets, to watch and record whenever police interacted with black people. At the time in California, it was legal to carry a gun. The program may have stopped some instances of police brutality, but it also led to violent clashes between the police and the BPP.

In addition, Bobby and the BPP played an important role in improving the health of black people. Bobby realized that public hospitals and clinics in black neighborhoods did not have enough money to take good care of their patients. Often, their staff members were disrespectful toward their black patients.

However, despite the good that the Panthers were doing, confrontations between them and the police continued. The BPP was investigated by the Federal Bureau of Investigation (FBI), which declared the organization to be an enemy of the government. Bobby was arrested and sentenced to one year of probation for fighting with police at an anti-war rally. In 1968, he was arrested again for protesting at the Democratic National Convention, where people had gathered to choose the presidential candidate for the Democratic party.

After years of conflict, Bobby instructed BPP members to focus more on their community work. In April 1970, Bobby instructed every BPP chapter to open healthcare clinics. They would be called People's Free Medical Clinics. The clinics would be safe and conveniently located and offer legal and housing services. The BPP opened 13 clinics across the country.

The Panthers began providing childcare and educational programs as well. They also served free breakfasts to children. The free breakfast program would be a positive legacy of the Black Panthers. The success of the breakfast program spurred the federal government to institute similar programs in public schools that still exist today.

However, violence continued to be associated with the Panthers. BPP members fought with each other and the police. Unsatisfied with the way things were going, Bobby decided to work for change from within the government. In 1973, he ran for mayor of Oakland. He was unsuccessful, but he continued helping the black community. In 1974, he quit the BPP.

After leaving the BPP, Bobby taught in the Africology and African American Studies Department at Temple University in Philadelphia, Pennsylvania. In 2002, he moved back to Oakland to help young activists bring about social change.

Today, Bobby's work continues. He has visited more than 500 colleges worldwide, giving lectures about his involvement with the BPP. However, his philosophy has changed from the days when he co-founded the BPP. He now encourages young activists to continue the fight to bring about equality and justice for all, but through peaceful means. "Always [have] a peaceful protest. Because you're exercising the First Amendment of the Constitution of the United States of America. It is the law of the land," he said.

Bobby exposed the strengths and the weaknesses of the mainstream civil rights movement. He also demonstrated that while violence might bring short-term victories, nonviolence can create lasting peace.

EXPLORE MORE! Bobby Seale has many interests: carpentry, architecture, and cooking, to name a few. If you are a budding chef, you might want to check out his cookbook, *Barbeque'n with Bobby.*

DID YOU KNOW? When Bobby Seale was eight, his family left Texas for California. Between 1915 and 1975, six million African Americans left the South to escape the Jim Crow laws that made life difficult and often dangerous. This became known as the Great Migration.

Glossary

abolish: To end or completely do away with

activist: A person who campaigns to bring about social or political change

African: Someone from the continent of Africa

assassinate: To kill a famous or public person for political reasons

black separatism: A political movement seeking separation of black people from white society to allow for their cultural and economic development

boarding school: A school at which the students live on campus and sleep in dormitories

boycott: To refuse to buy or use the services of a person or organization

brutality: Great cruelty; physical violence

chapter: The local branch or office of a large organization

Christian: Religion based on the life and teachings of Jesus of Nazareth

constitution: A set of rules that guides a country and explains the rights of citizens

custom: A traditional or accepted way of doing something

desegregate: To end a policy of separating groups by race

direct action: The use of strikes, boycotts, and sit-ins to protest something

discrimination: Treating a person unfairly because of race, sex, or other characteristics

doctrine: A set of beliefs held and taught be a religion, political party, or other group

eloquence: A powerful, moving, and persuasive way of talking

enslaved: Forced to work for no pay, to obey commands, and to live without personal freedom

European: Someone from the continent of Europe

fellowship: A friendly group or community of people who share interests

feminist: A person who supports equal rights for women

Indigenous: An ethnic group who has always lived in a particular place

indispensable: Essential, necessary, or required to make something happen

injustice: A wrong; an unfair act; lacking justice

integrate: To bring people with particular characteristics together in equal participation

Jim Crow laws: Laws in the South based on race that enforced segregation between white people and black people in public places and made it difficult for black people to vote

Ku Klux Klan: A racist organization that has terrorized black people since the days of slavery

legacy: Something received from the past

lynch: To kill someone without a trial, particularly by hanging

mainstream: Part of the ideas, attitudes, or activities that are considered normal or popular

martyr: A person killed because of their beliefs

mob violence: A group of people disturbing the peace by engaging in violence and other unlawful behavior

moral: Caring about doing the right thing

nonviolent: Using peaceful means rather than force, especially to bring about change

pacifist: Someone who believes that violence is never the answer

pastor: The minister in charge of a church or congregation

petition: A written request to an authority signed by many people

plantation: A large farm where crops were grown, often by slaves

politics: The set of activities involved in making decisions in groups or governments

prejudice: An opinion that is not based on reason or experience

racist: A person who is prejudiced against another person because of that person's race

reconciliation: The process by which two people or groups in a conflict come to an agreement

resistance: Refusal to agree or comply with something

resonate: To have particular meaning or importance

riot: A violent disturbance of the peace by a crowd

rural: An area in the countryside rather than the city that has open land and few houses

sawmill: A factory in which logs are sawed into lumber

second-class citizen: A person belonging to a social or political group that has fewer rights and opportunities than those of the dominant group in a society

segregation: The separation of people based on race or skin color

sit-in: A type of protest in which people enter a space, sit, and refuse to leave until their demands are met

slavery: The practice of selling, buying, and owning other human beings

unconstitutional: Something that is unlawful because it goes against an article in the U.S. Constitution

valedictorian: The graduating student who has the highest grade point average and who gives the farewell speech at the graduation ceremony

violence: Behavior involving physical force intended to hurt, damage, or kill someone or something

References

Adams, Russell L. *Great Negroes Past and Present*. Sacramento: California State Department of Education, 1973.

Albanese, Andrew. "ALA 2013: The Day Congressman John Lewis Got His Library Card." *Publisher's Weekly*. June 30, 2013. PublishersWeekly.com/pw/by-topic/digital/conferences/article/58040-ala-2013-the-day-congressman-john-lewis-got-his-library-card.html.

Bausum, Ann. *Freedom Riders: John Lewis and Jim Zwerg on the Front Lines of the Civil Rights Movement*. Washington, DC: National Geographic Kids, 2005.

Bausum, Ann. *The March Against Fear: The Last Great Walk of the Civil Rights Movement and the Emergence of Black Power*. Washington, DC: National Geographic Kids, 2017.

Biography.com Editors. "James Farmer." Biography.com. Last modified July 6, 2020. Biography.com/activist/james-farmer.

Black Issues. "Barnard College Honors Dorothy Height, 75 Years After Turning Her Away." *Diverse Issues in Higher Education*. July 1, 2004. DiverseEducation.com/article/3793.

Blain, Keisha N. "Fannie Lou Hamer's Dauntless Fight for Black Americans' Right to Vote." *Smithsonian Magazine*. August 20, 2020. SmithsonianMag.com/history/fannie-lou-hamers-dauntless-fight-for-black-americans-right-vote-180975610.

"Bobby Seale." My Black History. Accessed May 11, 2021. MyBlackHistory.net/Bobby_Seale.htm.

"Bobby Seale (October 22, 1936)." National Archives. African American Heritage. Accessed May 11, 2021. Archives.gov/research/african-americans/individuals/bobby-seale.

Burns, James MacGregor. *The Crosswinds of Freedom, 1932–1988*. Open Road Media, 2012.

Cantarow, Ellen, Susan Gushee O'Malley, and Sharon Hartman Strom. *Moving the Mountain: Women Working for Social Change*. New York: The Feminist Press of CUNY, 1993.

Coates, Ta-Nehisi. "The Legacy of Malcolm X." *The Atlantic*. May 2011. TheAtlantic.com/magazine/archive/2011/05/the-legacy-of-malcolm-x/308438.

Davis, Dernoral. "Medgar Evers and the Origin of the Civil Rights Movement in Mississippi." Mississippi Historical Society. *Mississippi History Now*. October 2003. MSHistoryNow.MDAH.MS.gov/articles/53/medgar-evers-and-the-origin-of-the-civil-rights-movement-in-mississippi.

"Dorothy Irene Height." NCNW. Accessed May 11, 2021. NCNW.org/ncnw/height.

Dunham, Montrew. *Thurgood Marshall: Young Justice*. New York: Simon and Schuster, 1998.

Encyclopedia of World Biography Editors. "Medgar Evers Biography." Accessed May 11, 2021. NotableBiographies .com/Du-Fi/Evers-Medgar.html#ixzz6rbA4zNLR.

Farmer, James. *Lay Bare The Heart: An Autobiography of the Civil Rights Movement*. New York: Arbor House, 1985.

Fraser, C. Gerald. "Ella Baker, Organizer for Groups for Civil-Rights Movement in South." *New York Times*. December 17, 1986. NYTimes.com/1986/12/17 /obituaries/ella-baker-organizer-for-groups-in-civil -rights-movement-in-south.html.

"Freedom Summer: Fannie Lou Hamer." Women in American History Collection. *American Experience*. PBS. Accessed May 11, 2021. PBS.org/wgbh /americanexperience/features/freedomsummer-hamer.

Gates Jr., Henry Louis, and Evelyn Brooks Higginbotham, eds. *African American Lives*. New York: Oxford University Press, 2004.

Height, Dorothy. "Civil Rights Elder Sees Dream Come True." Interview by Michel Martin. *Tell Me More*. NPR. November 6, 2008. NPR.org/templates/story/story.php? storyId=96694471.

History.com Editors. "Martin Luther King, Jr.'s Home is Bombed." History.com. Last modified January 27, 2021. History.com/this-day-in-history/martin-luther-king-jr-home-bombed-montgomery.

History.com Editors. "Montgomery Bus Boycott." History.com. Last modified January 27, 2021. History.com/topics/black-history/montgomery-bus-boycott.

History.com Editors. "Rosa Parks." History.com. Last modified January 12, 2021. History.com/topics/black-history/rosa-parks.

Hoose, Phillip. *Claudette Colvin: Twice Toward Justice.* New York: Farrar, Straus and Giroux, 2009.

Hourly History. *Martin Luther King Jr.: A Life from Beginning to End.* Kindle Edition. *Hourly History,* 2018.

Malcolm X, Alex Haley, and Attallah Shabazz. *The Autobiography of Malcolm X: As Told to Alex Haley.* New York: Ballantine Books, 1992.

"Medgar Evers." NAACP. Accessed May 11, 2021. NAACP.org/find-resources/history-explained/civil-rights-leaders/medgar-evers.

"Meredith March Against Fear, June 1966." Stanford Libraries. The Bob Fitch Photography Archive. Accessed May 11, 2021. Exhibits.Stanford.edu/fitch/browse/meredith-march-against-fear-june-1966.

Mills, Kay. "Fannie Lou Hamer: Civil Rights Activist." Mississippi Historical Society. *Mississippi History Now.* April 2007. MSHistoryNow.MDAH.state.MS.us/articles/51/fannie-lou-hamer-civil-rights-activist.

"Montgomery Bus Boycott." Stanford University. The Martin Luther King, Jr. Research and Education Institute. Accessed May 11, 2021. KingInstitute.Stanford.edu/encyclopedia/montgomery-bus-boycott.

Murray, Pauli. *Pauli Murray: The Autobiography of a Black Activist, Feminist, Lawyer, Priest, and Poet.* Knoxville: The University of Tennessee Press, 1989.

Nelson, Stanley. "'Policing the Police': How the Black Panthers Got Their Start." Interview by Terry Gross. *Fresh Air,* NPR. September 23, 2015. Audio, 37:54. WBUR.org/npr/442801731/director-chronicles-the-black-panthers-rise-new-tactics-were-needed.

Olson, Lynne. *Freedom's Daughters: The Unsung Heroines of the Civil Rights Movement from 1830 to 1970.* New York: Simon and Schuster, 2002.

"Pauli Murray." The Episcopal Diocese of North Carolina. Accessed May 11, 2021. Episdionc.org/pauli-murray.

Quigley, Eileen V. "Rights Leader, Bayard Rustin, 75, Dies: Pacifist Helped to Set Up King's March on Capital.

Los Angeles Times. August 25, 1987. LATimes.com/archives/la-xpm-1987-08-25-mn-4064-story.html.

Schulz, Kathryn. "The Many Lives of Pauli Murray." *The New Yorker*. April 17, 2017. NewYorker.com/magazine/2017/04/17/the-many-lives-of-pauli-murray.

Seeley, Katharine Q. "John Lewis, Towering Figure of Civil Rights Era, Dies at 80." *New York Times*. July 17, 2020. NYTimes.com/2020/07/17/us/john-lewis-dead.html.

"Thurgood Marshall." *Oyez*. Accessed May 11, 2021. Oyez.org/justices/thurgood_marshall.

Washington, James M., ed. *I Have a Dream: Writings and Speeches That Changed the World*. San Francisco: HarperCollins Publishers, 1993.

Weil, Ann. *Medgar Evers (American Biographies)*. Kindle Edition. Chicago: Heinemann, 2014.

Williams, Juan. "Men Changed by War Fight to Be Equals." *Washington Post*. July 26, 1995. WashingtonPost.com/archive/politics/1995/07/26/men-changed-by-war-fight-to-be-equals/ff719d33-91ab-4420-a88c-a038a33bcfc6.

Williams, Lea E. *We Who Believe in Freedom: The Life and Times of Ella Baker*. Charlotte, NC: J. Murrey Atkins Library at UNC Charlotte, 2017.

About the Author

Glenda Armand has had a long career in education. She has been an elementary school teacher and has taught English and history at the secondary level. She currently serves as a middle school librarian. She is the author of a number of picture book biographies, including *Love Twelve Miles Long*, *Ira's Shakespeare Dream*, and *Song in a Rainstorm: The Story of Musical Prodigy Thomas "Blind Tom" Wiggins*. Learn more at Glenda-Armand.com.

About the Illustrator

María Perera was born in a small seaside town in northern Spain. When she was young, she found out that there were few things in life that she enjoyed as much as listening to The Beatles and drawing. She graduated with a degree in art history, then studied graphic design. She has worked as a freelance illustrator for several international publishers and advertising agencies. She loves to spend time with her family and friends.